STRANGE
Life Cycles

The Bizarre Life Cycle of a
MAYFLY

By Greg Roza

Gareth Stevens
Publishing

Please visit our website, www.garethstevens.com. For a free color catalog of all our high-quality books, call toll free 1-800-542-2595 or fax 1-877-542-2596.

Library of Congress Cataloging-in-Publication Data

Roza, Greg.
The bizarre life cycle of a mayfly / Greg Roza.
    p. cm. — (Strange life cycles)
ISBN 978-1-4339-7052-8 (pbk.)
ISBN 978-1-4339-7053-5 (6-pack)
ISBN 978-1-4339-7051-1 (library binding)
1. Mayflies—Life cycles—Juvenile literature. I. Title. II. Series: Roza, Greg. Strange life cycles.
QL505.R69 2012
595.7'34—dc23
                              2011051764

First Edition

Published in 2013 by
Gareth Stevens Publishing
111 East 14th Street, Suite 349
New York, NY 10003

Copyright © 2013 Gareth Stevens Publishing

Designer: Andrea Davison-Bartolotta
Editor: Kristen Rajczak

Photo credits: Cover, pp. 1, 4, 7, 13, 18 Shutterstock.com; p. 5 Claude Robidoux/All Canada Photos/Getty Images; p. 8 iStockphoto/Thinkstock; p. 9 Mirko Zanni/WaterFrame/Getty Images; p. 11 Derzsi Elekes Andor/Wikimedia Commons; pp. 15, 19 iStockphoto.com; p. 17 Solvin Zankl/Visuals Unlimited/Getty Images; p. 20 David Woodfall/Stone/Getty Images.

Printed in the United States of America

CPSIA compliance information: Batch #CS12GS: For further information contact Gareth Stevens, New York, New York at 1-800-542-2595.

Contents

Words in the glossary appear in **bold** type the first time they are used in the text.

Swarm!

It's a warm night in late June. Suddenly, a giant **swarm** of mayflies approaches from a nearby lake. The strange bugs crowd around streetlights and rest on buildings. They even come into homes if windows aren't shut tight. Some mayfly swarms are so large they show up on weather **radar**! The next morning, however, they're gone.

The life cycle of a mayfly is truly bizarre. Most only live for about a year. Many mayflies live less than a day after they become adults.

THE FACTS OF LIFE

Mayflies belong to the scientific order Ephemeroptera (ih-feh-muh-RAHP-tuh-ruh). This word comes from the Greek words for "short lived" and "wings."

4

Meet the Mayflies

There are more than 2,000 species, or kinds, of mayflies. They live in and near water on every continent except Antarctica. More than 600 species live in North America.

Adult mayflies are easy to spot. They have one pair of large, triangle-shaped wings and one pair of smaller wings. They have a long body and six long legs. These features make them great flyers. If you see a mayfly sitting on a tree, you usually find hundreds more—often on the same tree!

THE FACTS OF LIFE

Most mayflies have three caudal filaments, or tails, at the end of their long body.

7

Life Begins Underwater

Mayfly eggs hatch in water. Recently hatched mayfly **larvae** are called nymphs. They're only about 0.04 inch (1 mm) long. Nymphs don't have wings like adult mayflies. However, most have a long body.

Shortly after hatching, the nymphs find something to hang on to. Different species act differently. Some tunnel into sand or mud. Some crawl between rocks. Others hang on to mossy rocks and plants. A few even swim freely in the water. They remain there for up to a year.

mayfly nymph

THE FACTS OF LIFE

Nymphs grow gills along the sides of their body. Gills allow the nymphs to breathe underwater.

Mayfly larvae are often found in fast-moving streams, but they may also live in lakes and ponds.

9

Molting Mayflies

Most mayfly nymphs eat the remains of plants and animals. Some eat live plants and **algae**. A few large species eat nymphs of smaller insects. Depending on the species, nymphs can grow to between 0.16 and 1.2 inches (4 and 30 mm) long.

As they grow, the nymphs **molt** many times. The number of molts is different for each species, but it ranges from 20 to 50 over the course of a year. The nymph increases in size with each molt.

THE **FACTS** OF **LIFE**

As nymphs grow, they become males or females. Males have very long front legs that they use when **mating**.

A young mayfly's body becomes more like an adult's with each molt.

Leaving the Water

For a nymph's final molt, some of its insides are emptied out of its body. Air replaces the guts, which are no longer needed since the insects won't eat again. Nymphs often let go of their underwater homes at about the same time and float to the water's surface.

When a nymph reaches the surface, its body cracks open and its wings **emerge**. The insect floats on the water until it's strong enough to fly. The mayfly—now called a subimago—has reached the first stage of adulthood.

THE FACTS OF LIFE

A mayfly's most dangerous time in life is when it floats on water as a new subimago. **Predators** eat many before they can fly away.

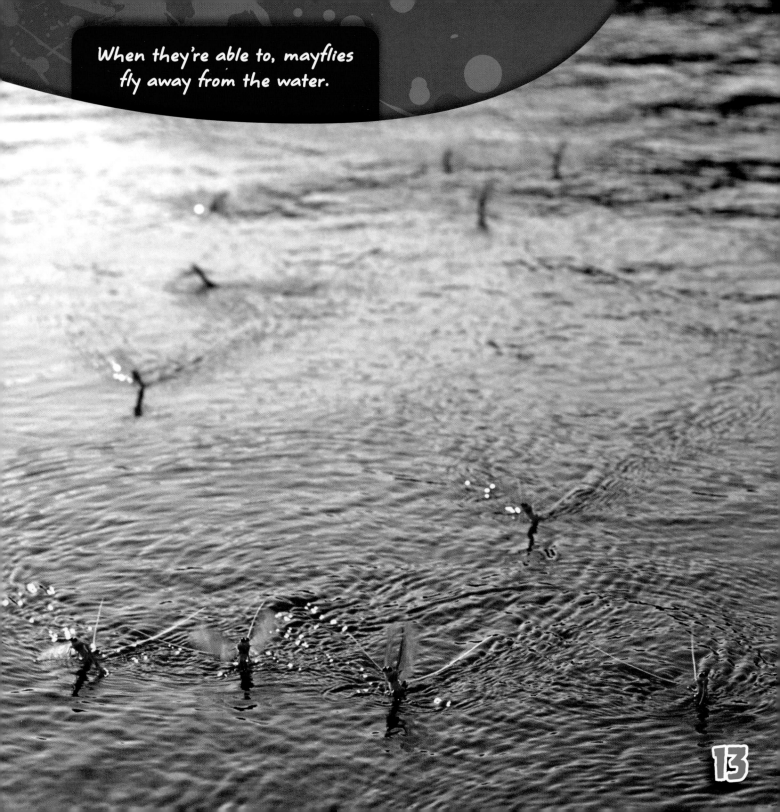

When they're able to, mayflies fly away from the water.

Still Growing

Unlike most insects, mayflies pass through two adult stages during their life cycle. As soon as the subimagos can fly, they leave the water for good. They swarm onto land to find new resting spots. These may be on a tree or long grass or under a bridge. Here they prepare to molt a last time.

The mayfly's final molt allows its legs and body to grow a little longer. After molting, the subimagos become imagos. By this time, they are fully mature and ready to mate.

THE FACTS OF LIFE

Mayflies are the only insects that molt again after their wings have formed.

This male mayfly has left behind its old skin to become an adult.

The End Is Near

Once male imagos are finished molting, they take off and swarm in the air. They're usually drawn to lights. In areas where mayflies are common, people often find dense clouds of them around streetlights.

Swarms of female imagos mix in with the male swarms. Males use their long front legs to hold females and mate with them. Then, each female spreads hundreds of eggs over water. Some release them directly into water. Soon after, the adult mayflies die.

THE FACTS OF LIFE

The time between the moment a subimago emerges from the water and the time the imago dies is less than 2 days. Often it's much shorter.

Some male mayflies mate within an hour of molting for the last time.

Mayflies for Dinner

Each female mayfly can lay up to about 1,200 eggs. This is important for mayfly **survival** because so many predators eat them. Mayfly eggs are eaten by snails and other insect larvae. Nymphs are **prey** for fish, frogs, birds, insects, and roundworms.

Adult mayflies don't eat. However, they're food for many other animals. Fish, birds, water beetles, and dragonflies eat many subimagos as they rest on the water's surface. Once a subimago leaves the water, it has far fewer predators to worry about.

mayfly fishing bait

THE FACTS OF LIFE

Fish love to snatch low-flying mayflies for a snack. Fly fishermen take advantage of this by using bait that looks like a mayfly.

Mayflies are quite beautiful up close!

19

Mayflies and People

Mayflies don't bite people or harm human property. However, they can be very annoying when they swarm. They can make driving difficult. A few days after a mayfly swarm passes through, their bodies can pile up in corners and on windowsills. Some people may be **allergic** to them. The piles often need to be cleared away with shovels!

Since most mayfly species don't grow well in polluted water and soil, large mayfly swarms are a sign of a healthy **environment**. They're also a great food source for other animals.

Fun Facts About Mayflies

- Mayflies are known by many different names, including Junebug, dayfly, fishfly, midge, and Canadian soldier.

- Subimagos are also known as duns. Imagos are called spinners.

- As you might have guessed from their long body, mayflies are related to dragonflies.

- The oldest-known, full-body fossil of a flying insect was recently found in Massachusetts. It's a mayfly! The fossil is 310 to 312 million years old.

- The largest mayflies have a body that's a little over 1 inch (2.5 cm) long. However, the tails of some species can be 3 inches (7.6 cm) long.

- Although mayflies are good fliers in calm weather, they're easily blown off course by wind and rain.

- Some reports say that Native Americans once ate mayfly larvae. Today, people on the island of Borneo eat adult mayflies in stir-fried dishes.

Glossary

algae: living plantlike things that are mostly found in water

allergic: having sensitivity to normally harmless things in the environment, such as dust, pollen, or mold

emerge: to come out

environment: the natural world

larvae: bugs in an early life stage that have a wormlike form. The singular form is "larva."

mate: to come together to make babies

molt: to shed old shells, skin, fur, or feathers while a new covering grows in

predator: an animal that hunts other animals for food

prey: an animal that is hunted by other animals for food

radar: a way of using radio waves to find distant objects

survival: the ability to stay alive

swarm: a large group of flying insects. Also, to fly in a large group.

For More Information

Books

Mound, Laurence. *Insect.* New York, NY: DK Publishing, 2007.

Parker, Steve. *Eyewitness: Pond & River.* New York, NY: DK Publishing, 2011.

Websites

Mayflies of the United States
www.npwrc.usgs.gov/resource/distr/insects/mfly/
Use an interactive map to see which mayfly species live in your county.

Mayfly Facts
www.mayflynews.net/facts.html
Learn much more about mayflies through facts, stories, photographs, and videos.

Index